ORIGAMI
Jewelry

ORIGAMI
Jewelry

A step-by-step guide to creating beautiful designs

Monika Cilmi

ARCTURUS

About the author

Monika Cilmi lives and works as a professional artist in Ipswich, UK. She has a BA in visual arts, a PG certificate in Japanese and Korean art, and has completed a Masters by Research in London, with a project called "Nature and the rituals of gesture." She has mounted exhibitions in Germany, Italy, Portugal, and England and collaborates with a dance company in Mexico. Monika is passionate about Japanese art and culture and her artwork expresses the harmony between logical research, emotion, and the instinctive application of practical skills. She has always been fascinated by paper and its myriad uses.

www.monikacilmi.com

ARCTURUS

This edition published in 2017 by Arcturus Publishing Limited
26/27 Bickels Yard, 151–153 Bermondsey Street,
London SE1 3HA

ISBN: 978-1-78428-769-6
AD005706US

Printed in China

Contents

Introduction 6

Hearts & Flowers 11
    Flower bracelet 12
    Bamboo brooch 14
    Hydrangea necklace 18
    Flower brooch 20
    Leaf bracelet 22
    Hearts brooch 24
    Geometric flower hairclip 26
    Elongated heart earrings 28
    Lotus brooch 30

Birds & Beasts 33
    Cat earrings 34
    Turtle bracelet 37
    Butterfly hairclip 40
    Elephant earrings 42
    Chick hairclip 44
    Fish necklace 46
    Fish bracelet 48
    Fox brooch 50
    Bird earrings 52
    Crane brooch..54

Spiky & Abstract 57
    Abstract necklace 58
    Contemporary bracelet...61
    Abstract earrings 64
    Abstract bracelet 66
    Diamond necklace 68
    Ethnic necklace 70
    Spiky gem necklace 72
    Spiky earrings...74

Geometric & Boxy 76
    Box earrings...77
    Boxes necklace 79
    Aerodynamic earrings...82
    Chain bracelet 85
    Piano earrings 88
    Japanese fan necklace 90
    Triangles necklace 92
    Triptych hairclip..94

Stockists 96

INTRODUCTION

I love origami and I love jewelry, so I've decided to combine the two! This book introduces the reader to origami jewelry inspired by traditional and contemporary styles of paper folding. Each project shows how to make the origami pieces, then demonstrates the way in which they can be transformed into necklaces, bracelets, earrings, brooches, and hairclips.

MATERIALS

Paper

Origami paper comes in different sizes, thicknesses and patterns. It's important to be precise when making origami for jewelry because the tiny elements mean you use smaller-sized paper than normal. If you are new to origami, perhaps start by practicing with 3½ x 3½in (9 x 9cm) or even bigger origami paper until you are confident about tackling the smaller sizes. Learning how to make a sharp crease is vital for producing neat and good-looking origami jewelry.

I recommend using medium-weight origami paper, too thick and the piece won't look elegant, too thin and it won't take the shape. Between 80 and 90gsm is a good weight.

Pliers

These are not essential, but can be useful for holding wire or other fiddly fixings.

Glue

You'll need to use glue to fix your pieces together. The best type is a clear, dry, and acid-free glue, which will not discolor the paper over time. Remember to use only a small amount. You can even use double-sided tape in some cases.

Coating

If you want to make your jewelry longer-lasting, you can use a waterproof coating such as clear nail polish or acrylic spray. It's always best to try different types because some can make the paper yellowish and create wrinkles. Apply two or three layers and remember to wait until each one dries before applying the next.

Beads

These come in a wide assortment of sizes, colors, and materials. Wood, plastic, glass, metal, or clay beads are all suitable.

FINDINGS

Earrings

Earring findings are available in a range of shapes and styles. Hooks are the most widely used finding, but certain types of earring require a post and clutch (a stud with a front and back).

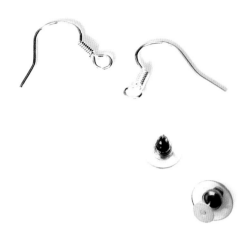

Necklaces and bracelets

Fine, coated nylon wire (or cord) is essential and can easily be found online. Stretchy cord is perfect for bracelets. You will need clasps to connect the jewelry; these come in a range of styles, including a round spring ring, a lobster claw, and a screw-on or magnetic clasp.

Brooches

For brooches, the only finding you should need is a bar pin, which is similar to a safety pin. These come in different lengths and are usually silver or gold in color.

Hairclips

The plain, metal type works best. I use barrette or snap clips, which are readily available online.

Introduction

FOLDS AND BASES

Mountain and valley folds

There are several important folds used in origami. Mountain and valley are simply the same fold, reversed. You either fold the top of the paper downward to form a mountain shape or the bottom edge upward to form a 'V' (valley) shape. Reverse folds are a little more tricky. Again, there are two main types: the inside reverse fold and the outside reverse fold.

Mountain fold

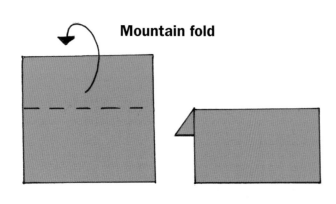

Valley fold

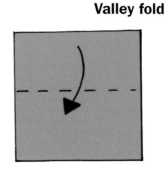
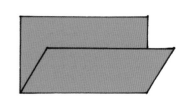

Inside reverse fold

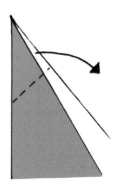

Outside reverse fold

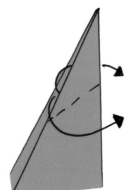
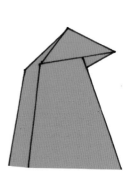

1 Fold your paper on the diagonal, then fold the tip along the dotted line. Fold in both directions to get a good crease.

2 Open the paper slightly and press the tip downward so it lies between the two sides. This is an inside reverse fold.

3 Crease the tip as before, but fold the sides of the paper outward along the crease.

4 Press down gently. This is an outside reverse fold.

Bird base

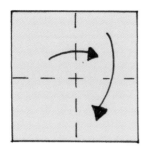

1 Fold the paper in half both ways. Open it up.

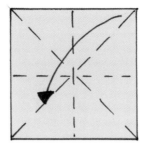

2 Fold the paper on the diagonal, both ways.

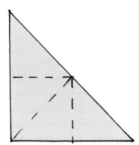

3 The shape will look like this.

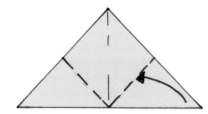

4 Rotate it so that the long folded side is at the bottom. Reverse fold the right corner so it is inside the shape.

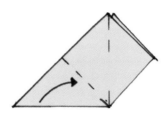

5 Reverse fold the left corner in the same way.

6 Your bird base should look like this.

Waterbomb base

1 Fold the paper in half, then in half again. Open it up.

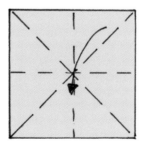

2 Fold the paper on the diagonal, both ways.

3 Open it up and fold in half again.

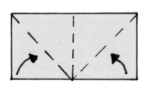

4 Rotate so that the long folded side is at the bottom. Reverse fold the right corner so it is inside the shape.

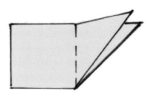

5 Reverse fold the left corner.

6 Your waterbomb base should look like this.

Introduction

Fish base

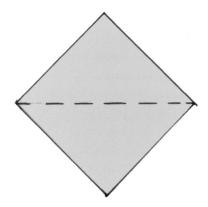

1 Fold the paper in half on the diagonal, then open it again.

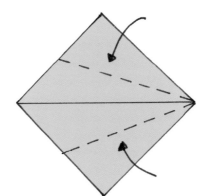

2 Fold inward along the dotted lines.

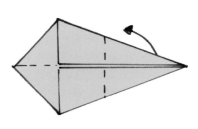

3 Mountain fold along the dotted line.

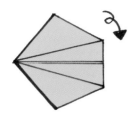

4 Turn the model over.

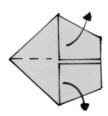

5 Start to open the flaps.

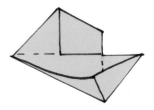

6 Gently press down and flatten one flap.

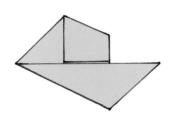

7 Your model should look like this.

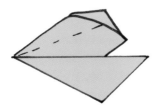

8 + 9 Now press down and flatten the other flap.

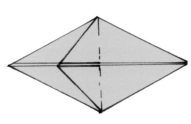

10 Lift the top flap and press it down. Turn the model over. Your fish base is ready to use.

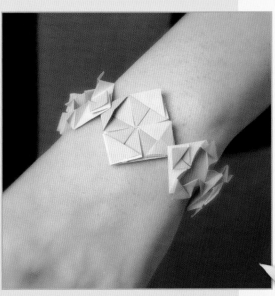

Hearts & Flowers

This section contains projects inspired by love and nature. I have used the origami heart design and various flowers to create necklaces, bracelets, brooches, and earrings. These pieces have a delicate shape and are ideal for celebrations, birthdays, or even Valentine's Day.

Flower bracelet

This pretty floral bangle looks great if created using double-sided paper.

Making the flowers

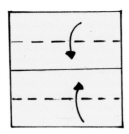

1 Start with the 2½in (7cm) square piece of paper. Fold it in half, reopen it, and fold along the dotted lines toward the center.

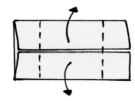

2 Reopen and fold in along the other two sides.

Materials

- 1 sheet of paper, 2½in (7cm) square
- 4 sheets of paper, 1½in (4cm) square
- a small lobster clasp
- a length of fine nylon cord (elasticized is best)
- glue
- a pin
- bugle beads

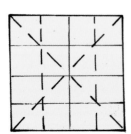

3 Fold on the diagonals.

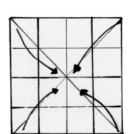

4 Reopen and fold all four corners to the center.

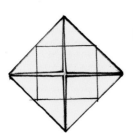

5 You should have created creases, like this.

6 Fold in along the dotted lines, pushing up the top right-hand corner (see next step).

7 Flatten the corner to make a small square.

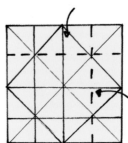

8 Do the same with the other three corners.

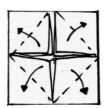

9 Fold down the top flap of each corner.

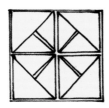

10 Now rotate the shape.

11 Your final design should look like this. You now need to make four more, using smaller origami paper, 4cm (1½in) square.

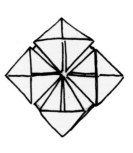

Making the bracelet

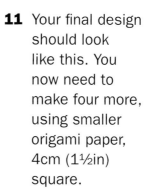

1 This is the structure you want to achieve.

2 Place the large origami flower in the center.

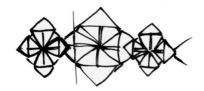

3 Place two smaller flowers on either side, gluing them together. Using a pin, make a small hole in each end of the last two flowers.

4 Attach a piece of cord on either side of the flower arrangement and thread with bugle beads.

5 Either tie the ends of the cord together (if elasticized) or add a small lobster clasp to finish.

Bamboo brooch

This stylish brooch looks best made with double-sided paper.

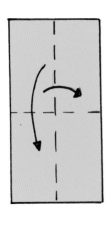

1 Fold the larger rectangle both ways, and reopen it.

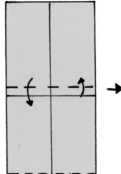

2 Fold the bottom of the paper underneath, along the dotted line. Fold the middle like an accordion, as shown.

3 Fold down the top corners along the dotted lines.

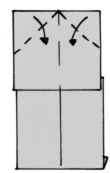

4 Fold the sides in to the center along the dotted lines, as shown.

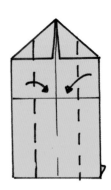

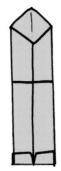

5 Your model will look like this. Reopen one side.

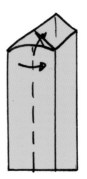

6 Fold up the top of the left-hand flap to make a straight crease, then close it. Do the same with the other flap.

Materials

- 2 rectangles of paper: the first 2½ x 4in (6 x 10cm) and the second 1½ x 3in (4 x 8cm)
- 4 sheets of paper, 1½in (4cm) square
- glue
- seed beads
- a bar pin

7 Fold the right-hand flap inside the left-hand one, closing the shape.

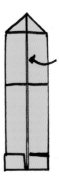

8 Model the shape gently to make it more rounded.

9 The stem should look like this. Now make another the same, using the smaller rectangle.

Making the leaves

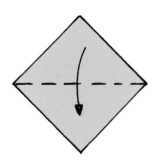

1 Using a square sheet of paper, fold down along the diagonal as shown.

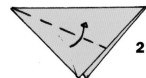

2 Fold up along the crease line.

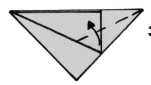

3 Fold up again along the crease line, as shown.

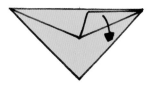

4 Fold down and open the right flap slightly.

5 Fold up and pull on the left, then flatten down.

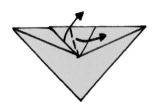

6 Fold up, opening the flap and pushing toward the right.

7 Fold along the lines and push in, folding down.

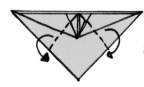

8 Fold behind along the dotted lines.

Bamboo brooch

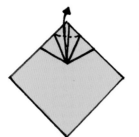

9 Fold up at the top. Turn the model over.

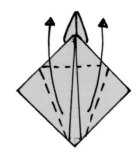

10 Fold up, pushing in the lateral flaps along the dotted lines.

11 Fold down along the dotted lines, as shown.

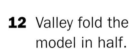

12 Valley fold the model in half.

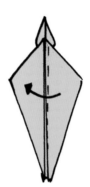

13 Fold down along the dotted lines, then do the same on the other side.

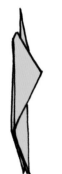 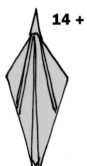

14 + 15 Unfold as in step 12 and open up the top flaps.

16 Your final design should look like this. Now make another three leaves exactly the same.

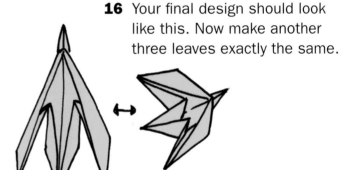

Making the brooch

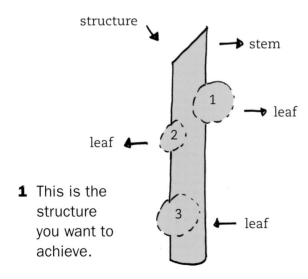

structure

stem

leaf

leaf

leaf

1 This is the structure you want to achieve.

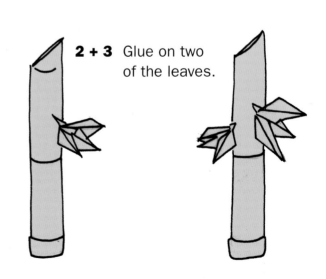

2 + 3 Glue on two of the leaves.

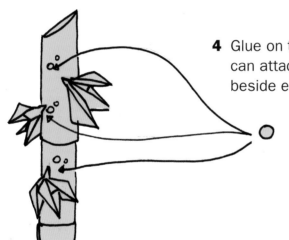

4 Glue on the third leaf. You can attach some tiny beads beside each leaf.

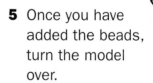

5 Once you have added the beads, turn the model over.

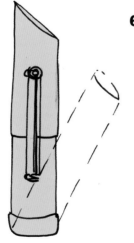

6 Add one leaf to the second smaller stem and glue this to the back of the larger stem. Add the bar pin, gluing it to the back of the larger stem.

Hydrangea necklace

This flower necklace is easy to make, but effective all the same, and works best made with double-sided paper that is patterned on one side.

Making the flowers

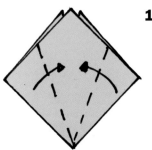

1 Using one of the sheets of paper, start with a bird base open at the top. Fold in along the dotted lines, as shown.

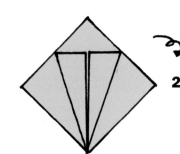

2 Turn the model over and do the same on the other side.

3 Fold up along the dotted line.

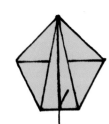

4 Fold down again to leave a crease.

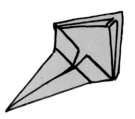 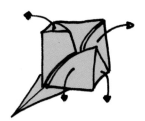

5 + 6 Start to open the top, pulling out the four petals.

7 Flatten the petals slightly, but not too much, to give a realistic look. Now make the other four flowers.

Materials

- *2 sheets of paper 1½in (4cm) square*
- *3 sheets of paper 2in (5cm) square*
- *glue*
- *a pin*
- *a length of fine nylon cord*
- *seed beads*
- *bugle beads*
- *a magnetic clasp*

Making the necklace

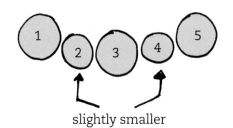

slightly smaller

1 This is the structure you want to aim for—alternating the larger and smaller flowers.

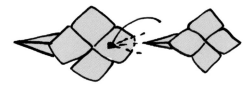

2 Glue the flowers together.

glued parts

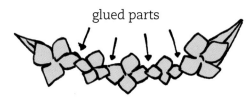

3 Glued together, the five flowers should create a slightly curved shape.

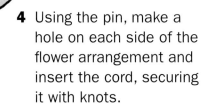

4 Using the pin, make a hole on each side of the flower arrangement and insert the cord, securing it with knots.

5 Thread ten seed beads on the cord, then one bugle bead, then another ten seed beads. Do this on both sides of the flowers. Attach a magnetic clasp.

6 The final piece should look like this.

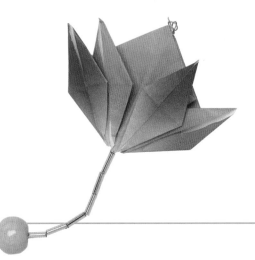

Flower brooch

This piece is inspired by a Japanese diagram, but I've added a twist to the design. You can use any type of paper, though a patterned or graduated-color paper is best.

Making the flower

1 Start with the waterbomb base.

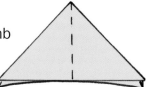

2 Fold up the top flaps along the dotted lines.

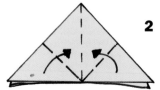

3 Open the left-hand flap.

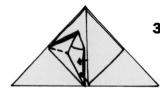

4 Press it down so that it makes a small square.

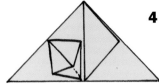

5 Do the same with the right-hand flap.

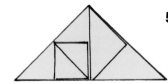

6 On the small square, fold in the flaps along the dotted lines.

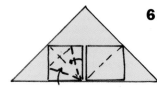

7 Do the same on the other side.

8 Open up the folds you have just made, lift the flap, and flatten it into a diamond shape (*see detail, left*).

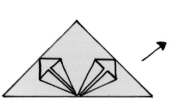

Materials

- *1 sheet of paper 8cm (3in) square*
- *a needle*
- *a length of fine nylon cord*
- *bugle beads*
- *a round bead*
- *a bar pin*

9 The shape should look like this.

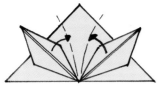

10 Fold along the dotted lines to bring the two shapes closer together.

11 Repeat steps 2–9, working on the flaps behind the ones you have just made . . .

12 . . . like this.

13 Your final piece should look like this.

Making the brooch

1 Using the needle, make a small hole in the centre top.

2 Thread the needle with cord and pass it through the hole and out of the model at the base. Knot the end (this will not be very visible).

3 Thread bugle beads on the cord 'stem' and finish with a round bead. I've used a wooden bead, but any type would work. Knot the cord at the end to secure the beads.

4 Glue the bar pin to the reverse of the brooch.

Leaf bracelet

This delicate piece is lovely made with double-sided or washi paper.

Making the leaves

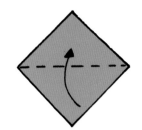

1 Fold your square of paper along the diagonal.

Materials

- *7 sheets of paper 1in (3cm) square*
- *a needle*
- *a length of satin cord*
- *seed beads*
- *a barrel, spring ring, or lobster clasp*

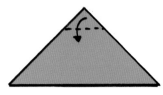

2 Fold down along the dotted line.

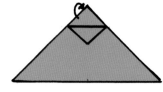

3 Fold the other tip behind.

4 Fold up along the dotted line.

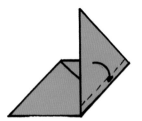

5 Now fold down along the dotted line, making a mountain fold.

6 Fold up along the dotted line and then down again so you have two mountain folds.

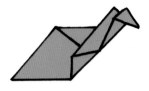

7 Your model should look like this. Turn it over.

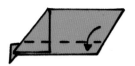

8 Fold down along the dotted line.

9 Now fold up.

10 Reopen to see all the creases made (they should be clearly visible).

11 Fold up along the dotted line.

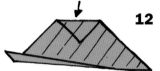

12 Open from the top to reveal the color on the reverse.

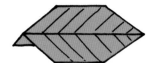

13 Rotate and model the leaf at the corners to give a rounded shape.

14 The leaf should look like this. Make another six of these.

Making the bracelet

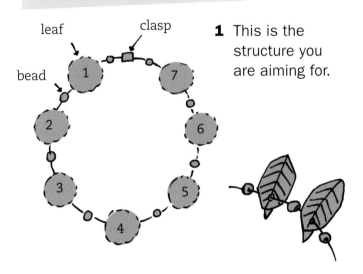

leaf   clasp

bead

1 This is the structure you are aiming for.

2 With the needle, make a hole at the same point on each of the leaves.

3 Thread the cord through a leaf and knot it. Add a seed bead and knot the cord again.

4 Continue in this way, inserting a bead between each leaf. Keep the elements reasonably close together so that the bracelet holds firm.

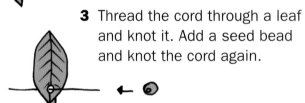

spring ring clasp

lobster claw clasp

5 Choose your preferred type of clasp and secure it with knots.

6 The final bracelet should look like this.

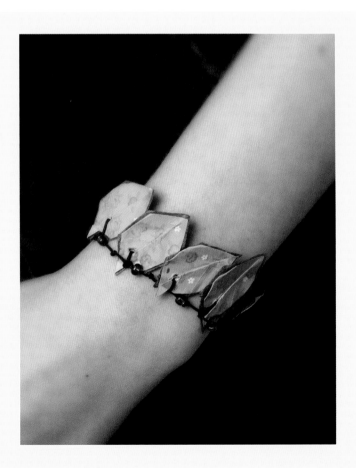

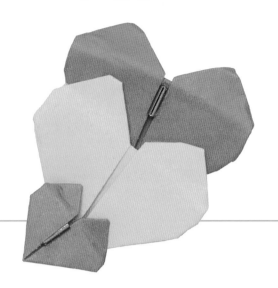

Hearts brooch

This lovely open-hearted design can be created with any type of traditional origami paper, but red and pink work best, of course!

Making the hearts

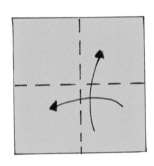

1 Take one of the larger squares of paper and fold both ways along the dotted lines. Leave it folded in half.

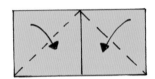

2 Fold down along the dotted lines towards the center.

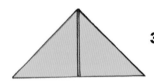

3 Turn the model over.

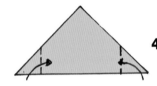

4 Fold inward along the dotted lines.

5 Your model should look like this. Turn it upside down.

6 Fold down along the dotted line.

7 Open the top flaps on both sides and press down.

8 Fold down the two small flaps along the dotted lines.

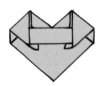

9 Turn the model over.

Materials

- 2 sheets of paper 2½in (7cm) square, one red, one pink
- 1 sheet of red paper 1½in (4cm) square
- bugle beads
- glue or double-sided tape
- a bar pin

10 To make a more rounded shape, model each corner with your fingers.

11 Here is the finished heart. Make two more, using the remaining sheets of paper.

Making the brooch

1 The hearts are arranged in this sequence.

2, 3 + 4 Glue the hearts together on the slant to give an elegant curved effect.

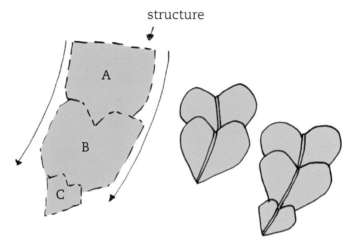

structure

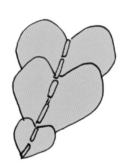

5 Glue bugle beads to the center of each heart in a continuous line.

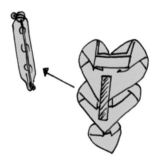

6 Using glue or double-sided tape, attach the bar pin to the reverse of the model.

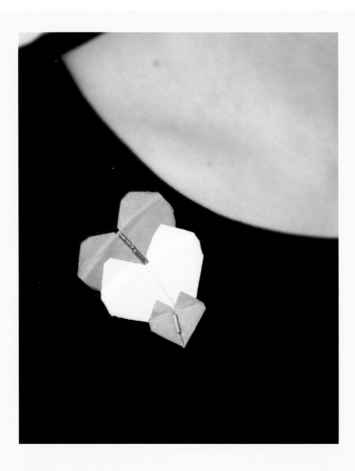

Geometric flower hairclip

This design looks great using patterned paper.

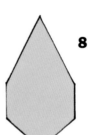

Making the decoration

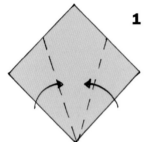

1 Take the 2in (5cm) square sheet of paper and fold inward along the dotted lines.

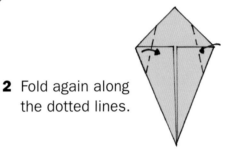

Materials

- 1 sheet of paper, 2in (5cm) square
- 3 sheets of paper, 1in (2.5cm) square
- glue
- a barrette or snap clip

2 Fold again along the dotted lines.

3 Turn it over.

4 This is the first part of the decoration (A).

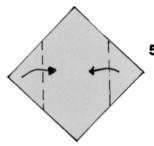

5 Take a 1in (2.5cm) square of paper and fold along the lines as shown.

6 Fold inward again along the dotted lines, as shown.

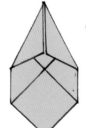

7 The shape looks like this.

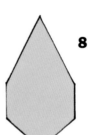

8 Turn it over. Make two of these shapes (B).

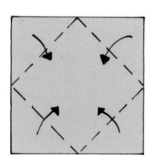

9 Take the final square of paper and fold all the corners to the center.

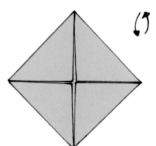

10 Rotate so that the model is square on and turn it over.

11 Fold the corners to the center.

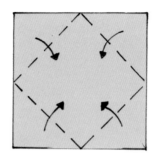

12 Your final piece should look like this (C).

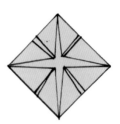

Assembling the hairclip

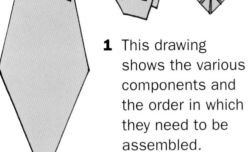

1 This drawing shows the various components and the order in which they need to be assembled.

2 Glue the two shapes B onto shape A, as shown.

3 Glue shape C onto shapes B.

4 Glue the assembled origami piece to the clip. If you find it difficult to glue directly to the metal, glue a piece of paper to the top of the clip and fix the origami model to this.

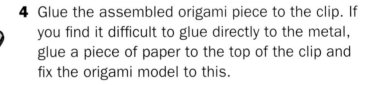

Elongated heart earrings

Two designs in one produce a unique piece which works well with any colorful origami or patterned paper.

Making the origami shapes

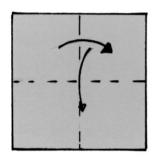

1 Use the 1½in (4cm) square sheets to make two heart shapes (see pages 24–5 for instructions). Take one of the 2½in (6cm) square sheets, fold it in half twice as shown and reopen it.

Materials

- 2 sheets of paper 1½in (4cm) square
- 2 sheets of paper 2½in (6cm) square
- glue
- a needle
- a short length of satin cord
- seed beads
- wire earring hooks

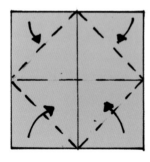

2 Fold in the corners along the dotted lines.

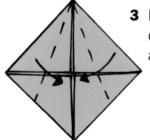

3 Fold along the dotted lines, as shown.

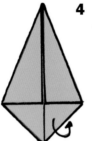

4 Fold the bottom triangle behind the model.

5 Valley fold the model in half.

6 The piece should look like this. Make another the same and turn them upside down to make the earrings.

Making the earrings

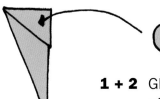

1 + 2 Glue the heart shape to the top of the second shape, as shown, and make a hole in the top of the model with a needle.

3 Thread the cord through the hole and add three or four beads. Secure with knots.

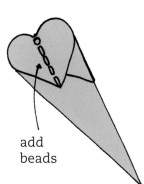

add beads

4 Fix the cord to an earring hook with a knot. Do the same with the second earring.

Lotus brooch

This lotus flower and leaf brooch combines two designs. It works best with traditional origami or washi paper.

Materials

· 2 sheets of paper, 2in (5cm) square, 1 red, 1 green
· glue
· a bar pin

Making the flower

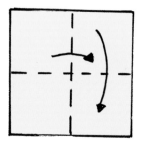

1 Fold the red sheet of paper in half both ways along the dotted lines and reopen it.

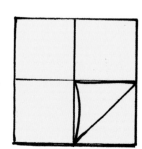

2 Fold each corner toward the center.

3 + 4 Turn the model over and fold each corner in again.

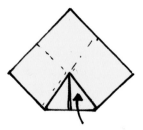

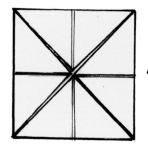

5 Turn the model over.

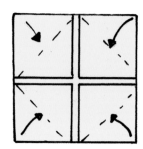

6 Fold all the corners in again.

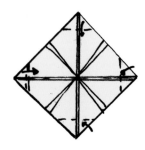

7 + 8 Fold in about a quarter of each corner to create the lotus shape.

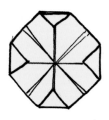

9 Open each flap, hold it from behind, then fold it on the other side to create a round shape with four petals.

10 The final piece should look like this.

Making the leaf

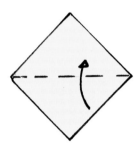

1 Fold the green paper in half on the diagonal and reopen it.

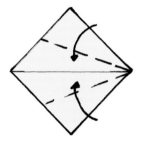

2 Fold in along the dotted lines.

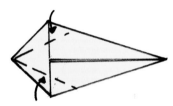

3 Fold along the dotted lines again.

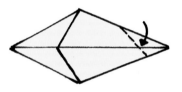

4 Make a crease and fold down along the dotted line.

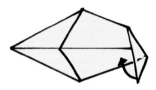

5 Make another smaller crease and fold up.

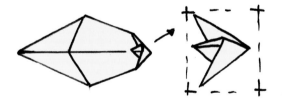

6 Make sure the middle triangle aligns with the center of the model.

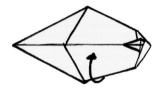

7 Valley fold it in half.

Lotus brooch

8 Rotate the model.

9 + 10 Starting on the left, fold along the length of the leaf, like an accordion, then open it out.

Assembling the brooch

1 Glue the flower onto the leaf.

2 Attach a bar pin to the reverse.

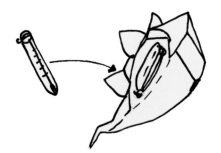

3 The brooch is ready to wear!

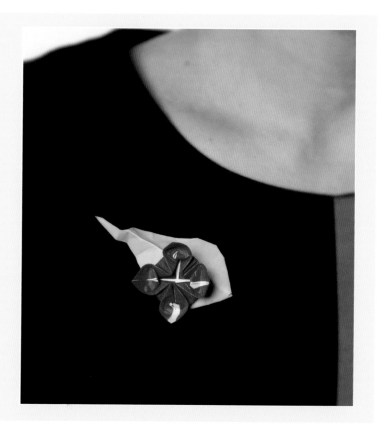

Birds & Beasts

This section includes projects inspired by birds and animals. It features single and modular designs applied to a range of jewelry concepts. Several of the designs are quirky, others are elegant—there is something here for everyone!

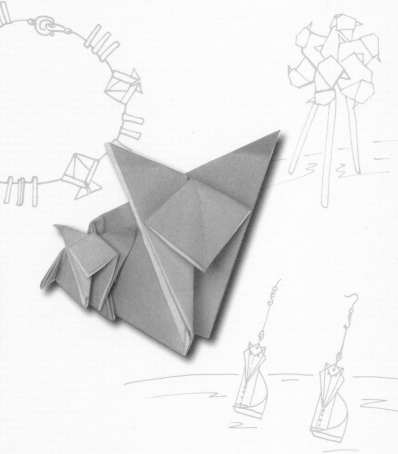

Cat earrings

This intriguing design is best created with double-sided paper (ideally black and white).

Making the cat

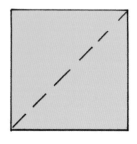

1 Fold your paper in half along the diagonal and reopen.

Materials

- *2 sheets of paper, 1.5in (4cm) square*
- *a pin*
- *2 metallic spiral beads*
- *a short length of satin cord*
- *wire earring hooks*
- *glue (optional)*
- *seed beads (optional)*

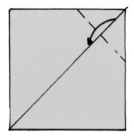

2 Fold the top corner down along the dotted line and unfold. Fold the sheet along the diagonal again.

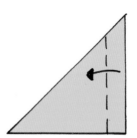

3 Fold the side inward along the dotted line.

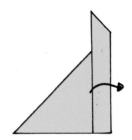

4 Unfold again.

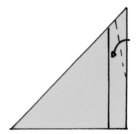

5 Fold along the dotted line and reopen.

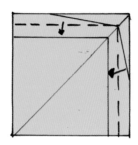

6 Fold in along the dotted lines then turn the model over. If you are using black and white paper, the black side should be on top.

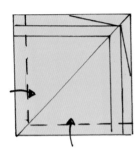

7 Fold along the dotted lines and turn the model over (the white side will now be on top).

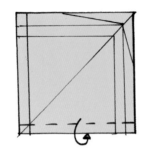

8 Fold the paper behind along the dotted line.

9 Fold the model in half along the diagonal (the black side will be on top).

10 Flatten down the left-hand corner.

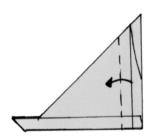

11 Open up the right-hand side along the dotted line.

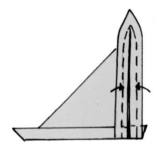

12 Fold in toward the center along the dotted lines.

13 Fold the top part down to make the cat's head, using all the creases created earlier.

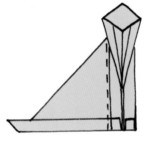

14 Turn the model over and fold back along the line on the left.

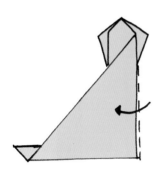

15 Turn the model over again.

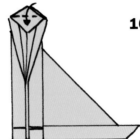

16 Fold the top point down and turn the model over.

Cat earrings

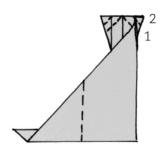

17 Fold along the dotted lines as follows: 1, fold down; 2, fold up. This should give an accordion pleat. Turn the model over and fold inward along the dotted line.

18 Your final design will look like this. Make another cat exactly the same.

Making the earrings

1 Using a pin, create a hole in the cat's head. Thread the cord through.

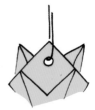

2 Thread both ends of the cord through a metallic spiral bead—this will keep the cord in place.

3 Tie the cord to an earring hook and finish off neatly. If you like, you can glue some seed beads along the cat's body; use two for the eyes. Make another earring exactly the same.

Turtle bracelet

This quirky design is very effective and looks lovely created with either double-sided or patterned paper.

Making the turtle

Materials

- 6 sheets of paper, 1½in (4cm) square
- scissors
- a length of satin or elastic cord
- a needle
- 5 round wooden beads
- a round spring or magnetic clasp (optional)

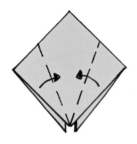

1 Start with a bird base, open at the bottom. Fold the top flap toward the center along the dotted lines.

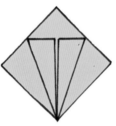

2 Turn the model over and do the same on the reverse.

3 Open the flaps and lift the bottom corner.

4 Gently flatten down the shape.

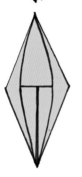

5 Do the same on the other side to create a diamond shape. Rotate it 180 degrees.

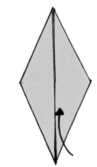

6 The divided flaps should be at the top. Lift the bottom flap.

7 Accordion pleat the tip of the flap, as shown.

8 Inside reverse fold the divided flaps to make the front flippers, as shown.

Turtle bracelet

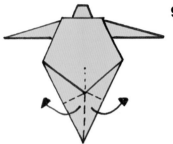

9 Using the scissors, cut up from the base. Fold the two back flippers under along the dotted lines.

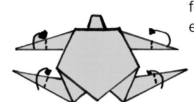

10 Inside reverse fold the tip of each flipper.

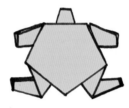

11 The final design should look like this. Make another five turtles exactly the same.

Making the bracelet

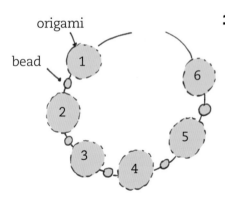

origami

bead

1 This is the structure you want to achieve. The number of turtles can vary depending on the size of bracelet you want. Six turtles will make a small/medium-sized bracelet.

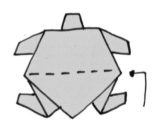

2 Thread the needle with satin cord and pull it through the center of the turtle.

3 Add a small wooden bead either side of the turtle.

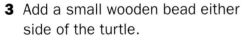

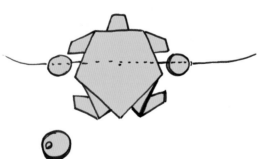

4 Continue threading beads and turtles until you have used them all. Knot the cord after the final bead to keep everything in place.

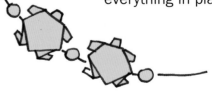

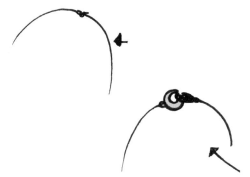

5 For the fitting, you can use either an elastic cord and tie the ends together or attach a clasp, as shown.

6 Your final bracelet will look like this.

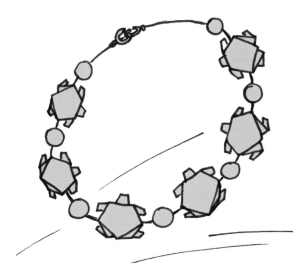

Butterfly hairclip

This insect-inspired design looks great created with patterned or washi paper.

Making the body

1 Fold a sheet of paper in half along the diagonal.

2 Open it.

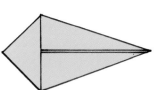

3 Fold both flaps toward the center along the dotted lines.

4 Your piece should look like this. Turn it over.

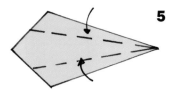

5 Fold both flaps toward the center along the dotted lines.

6 Mountain fold the model down the center and rotate it 90 degrees.

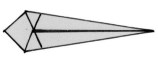

7 Crease along the dotted line and outside reverse fold the tip.

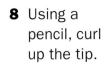

8 Using a pencil, curl up the tip.

Materials

- 2 sheets of paper, 2¾in (7cm) square
- a pencil
- glue
- a barrette or snap clip

9 Your final model for the butterfly body should look like this.

Making the wings

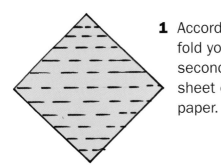

1 Accordion fold your second sheet of paper.

2 Open it out a little and pinch in the middle.

3 The final design for the butterfly wings looks like this.

Making the hairclip

2 . . . like this.

1 Glue the wings between the flaps on the back of the body . . .

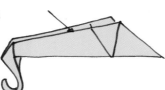

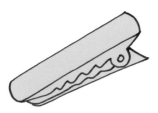

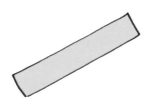

3 Glue the butterfly to the back of the barrette or snap clip. If you prefer, you can cut a piece of paper to glue to the back of the clip before adding the origami model.

Elephant earrings

This simple yet eye-catching design looks lovely made with colored or patterned paper—it doesn't have to be gray!

Making the elephant

Materials

- *2 sheets of paper, 1½in (4cm) square*
- *scissors*
- *a pin*
- *a length of fine nylon cord*
- *bugle or assorted beads*
- *wire earring hooks*

1 Fold a sheet of paper in half along the diagonal.

2 Reopen it.

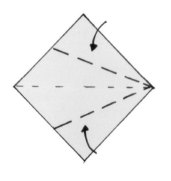

3 Fold both sides to the center along the dotted lines.

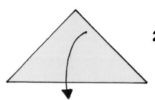

4 Valley fold the model in half.

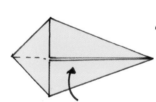

5 Rotate the model 180 degrees.

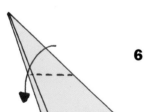

6 Crease both ways along the dotted line.

7 Make an outside reverse fold as shown.

8 The model should look like this.

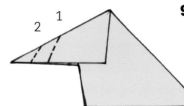

9 Press down so that the head is at the angle shown. Make two creases along the dotted lines.

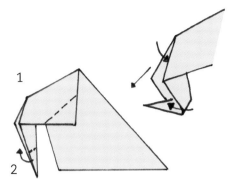

10 Make two inside reverse folds—the first one down, the second one up (*see detail*). Make creases for the ears along the dotted line.

11 With scissors, cut along the dotted lines to make the legs and tail.

12 Your final model looks like this. Make another elephant exactly the same.

Making the earrings

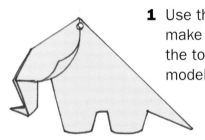

1 Use the pin to make a hole at the top of your model.

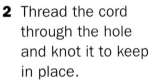

2 Thread the cord through the hole and knot it to keep in place.

3 Thread two beads onto the cord—you can use different shapes if you like.

4 Tie the cord to an earring hook. Repeat these steps with the second earring.

5 Here are some examples of different bead options.

Chick hairclip

This modular shape can be created with colored or patterned paper.

Making the chick

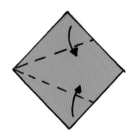

1 Fold the sides of the paper to the center along the dotted lines.

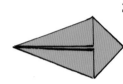

2 The model will look like this. Turn it over.

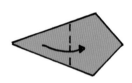

3 Fold in along the dotted line.

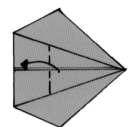

4 Fold out along the dotted line.

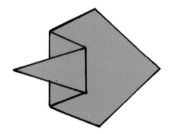

5 Turn the model over.

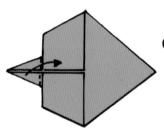

6 Fold the tip forward.

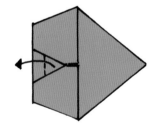

7 Fold the end of the tip down along the dotted line.

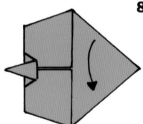

8 Mountain fold the model in half.

Materials

· 7 sheets of paper, 2½in (6cm) square
· glue
· scissors
· a snap clip

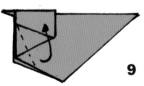

9 Crease along the dotted line and make an inside reverse fold.

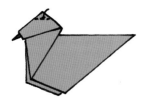 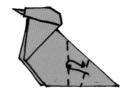 

10 Inside reverse fold the top of the head along the dotted line, and rotate the shape slightly.

11 Crease both ways along the dotted lines and make an inside reverse fold to create the tail.

12 Your final design should look like this. Make five more chicks exactly the same.

Making the hairclip

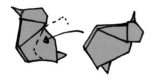

1 Carefully glue the chicks one on top of the other. You want to make a circle, so glue them at a slight angle.

2 Once you have made your circle, cut three strips of paper with rounded ends. One should be longer than the other two. Glue these to the back of the chicks.

3 Glue your model to a snap clip.

4 The finished piece should look like this.

Fish necklace

This design is inspired by 3D origami and looks effective with brightly colored or, possibly, graduated-color paper.

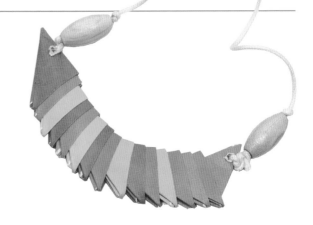

Making the fish

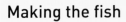

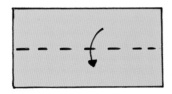

1 Fold a sheet of paper in half downward along the dotted line.

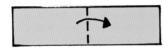

2 Fold in half, then open it again.

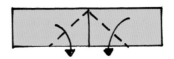

3 Fold both sides down along the dotted lines.

4 The model will look like this. Turn it over and rotate 180 degrees.

5 Fold down the corners along the dotted lines.

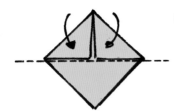

6 Valley fold the model in half along the dotted line.

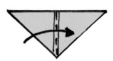

7 Fold it in half again from left to right.

8 This is the final piece. Now make 14 more.

Materials

- 15 rectangular sheets of paper, 1½ x 3in (4 x 7.5cm)
- glue
- a needle
- a length of satin cord
- wooden beads
- a magnetic clasp

Making the necklace

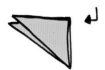

1 Position the first piece like this. It has two pockets at the back.

2 Insert the second piece into the first, as shown. Each point should go into one of the pockets.

3 Continue linking your pieces together until you are left with just one. The final piece is positioned differently (*see left*). The pieces should be secure, but you can put a little glue between them if you like.

4 Using the needle, make a hole and thread satin cord through each end of the model. Tie off neatly.

5 Thread one large or several small beads on either side of the model and add a magnetic clasp, securing with small knots.

Fish bracelet

This design is the essence of simplicity but produces an effective, solid shape. It looks good created with delicate pastel-colored or patterned paper.

Making the fish

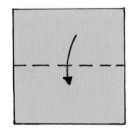

1 Fold a sheet of paper in half along the dotted line.

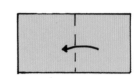

2 Fold in half again, then reopen it.

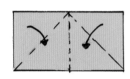

3 Fold down along the dotted lines, as shown.

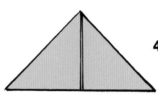

4 The model should look like this.

5 Open one flap.

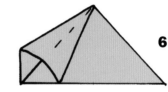

6 Gently press the flap down.

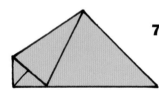

7 Do the same on the other side.

8 Fold each flap in half behind, along the dotted lines.

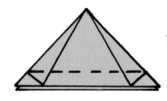

9 Fold the model up along the dotted line. Turn it over and do the same on the other side. One flap folds in front, the other folds behind.

Materials

- 5 sheets of paper, 1½in (4cm) square
- scissors
- glue
- a length of satin cord
- a round clasp

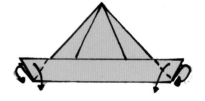

10 Fold down the two small flaps at each end.

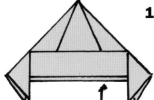

11 Open the bottom of the model and gently press it down into a rhombus shape.

12 The finished model looks like this. Make three more fish exactly the same.

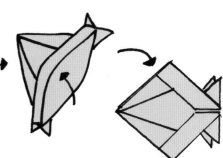

Making the bracelet

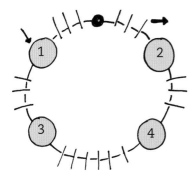

1 This is the structure you want to achieve. The fish are alternated with strips of origami paper.

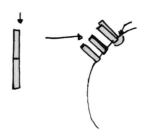

2 Cut 18 strips of paper, 1in (2.5cm) long and ⅛in (3mm) wide. Dab a little glue to the reverse of a strip and fold it over the length of cord, pressing together. Attach six strips of paper in this way. Make sure they are evenly spaced.

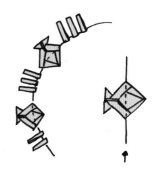

3 Thread a fish onto the cord. Add three more strips on either side of the fish; then add two more fish.

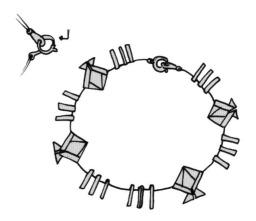

4 Tie the ends of the cord to a round clasp. Finish off neatly.

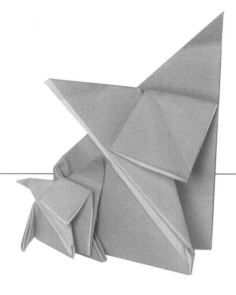

Fox brooch

This little design has an abstract feel and should be made using double-sided origami paper.

Materials

- 1 sheet of paper, 2¾in (7cm) square
- 1 sheet of paper, 1in (2.5cm) square
- glue
- a bar pin

Making the fox

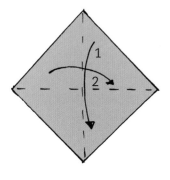

1 Taking the larger sheet of paper, fold down along the diagonal and reopen it. Then fold along the second diagonal.

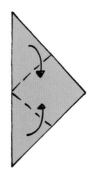

2 Fold in along the dotted lines.

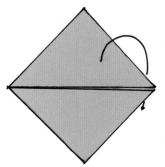

3 You should now have this shape. Mountain fold it in half.

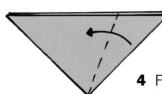

4 Fold the top flap along the dotted line.

5 Open the flap and press down gently.

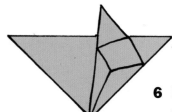

6 Rotate the model slightly.

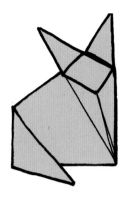

7 Fold in the tail. Your mother fox is ready.

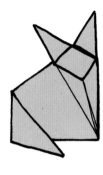

8 With the smaller sheet of paper, make a baby fox in exactly the same way.

Making the brooch

1 Glue the small fox on top of the larger one, as shown.

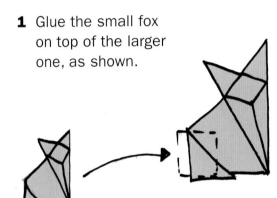

2 Glue a bar pin to the reverse. Your fox brooch is complete.

Bird earrings

These earrings are an interesting shape and make a great gift for bird lovers. They work well with double-sided patterned paper or washi paper.

Making the bird

1 Fold a sheet of paper on the diagonal, then reopen and fold both sides to the center along the dotted lines.

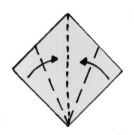

Materials

- *2 sheets of paper, 2in (5cm) square*
- *scissors*
- *a pin*
- *a length of fine nylon cord*
- *seed beads*
- *wire earring hooks*

2 Fold the top triangle behind, as shown.

3 Fold down along the dotted lines.

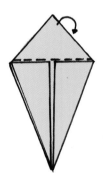

4 Reopen your last folds one at a time.

5 Crease as shown. Pull open the flap and press down, being careful to follow the creases.

6 Do the same with the other flap.

7 Fold up the points.

8 Valley fold to close the shape. Flip and rotate it 90 degrees.

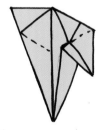

9 Crease both ways along the dotted line and inside reverse fold the head. Pull out the beak slightly.

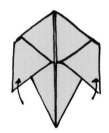

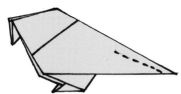

10 With scissors, cut along the dotted line and fold up the wings on either side.

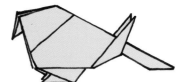

11 The final piece should look like this. Make another bird exactly the same.

Making the earrings

1 Using the pin, make a hole for the cord (it will look like the bird's eye).

2 Thread the cord through the hole and add three beads—they can be any shape you like.

3 Add and secure an earring hook. Make another earring in exactly the same way.

knot

Crane brooch

This version of the classic origami crane model is an intricate piece. It works well with any good-quality origami paper.

Making the crane

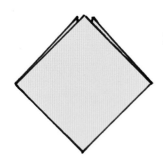

1 Start with a bird base.

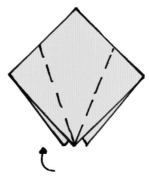

2 Rotate so that it is open at the bottom, and crease along the dotted lines.

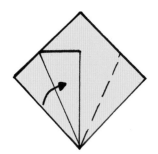

3 Fold the front flaps in to the center.

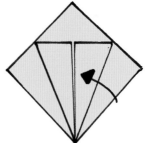

4 Turn over and do the same on the reverse.

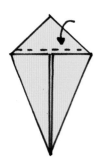

5 Fold down the top triangle along the dotted line.

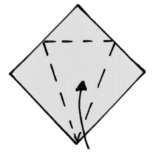

6 Reopen the flaps and pull up from the bottom point.

Materials

- 4 sheets of paper, 2in (5cm) square
- 1 sheet of paper, 1in (2.5cm) square
- glue or double-sided tape
- a pin
- a length of fine nylon cord
- seed beads
- a bar pin

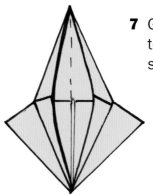

7 Gently flatten to make this shape.

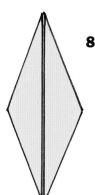

8 Turn over and repeat on the reverse.

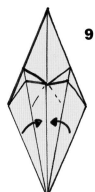

9 Fold both flaps in half toward the center.

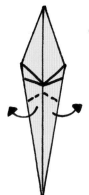

10 Turn over and do the same on the reverse. Then fold up along the dotted lines.

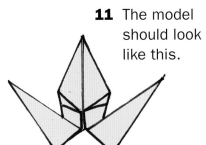

11 The model should look like this.

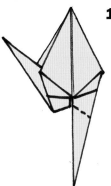

12 Fold the flaps down again and inside reverse fold them, as shown.

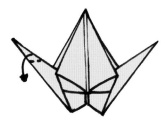

13 Crease the tip both ways and inside reverse fold to make the head.

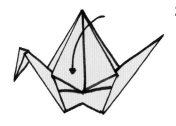

14 Finally, fold down the wings so that they are slightly open. Make another three cranes like this. Make a final crane with the smaller sheet of paper.

Making the brooch

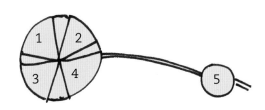

1 This is the structure you want to achieve.

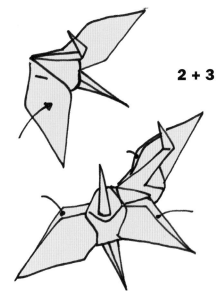

2 + 3 Add some glue or double-sided tape to the underside of the wings and join all four large cranes together.

Crane brooch

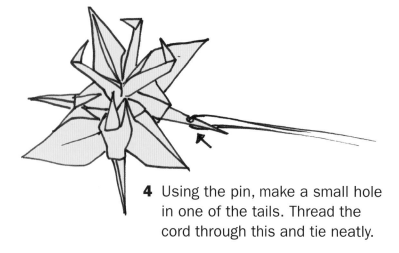

4 Using the pin, make a small hole in one of the tails. Thread the cord through this and tie neatly.

5 Add some small beads—squares or rectangles look good. You'll need about ten.

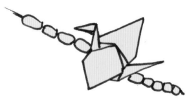

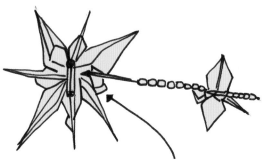

6 Pass the cord through the small origami crane, then add five more beads. Secure the cord with knots.

7 Glue a bar pin to the reverse.

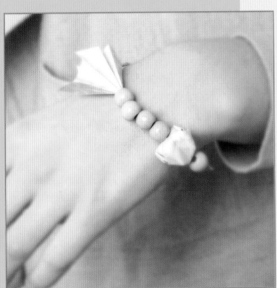

Spiky & Abstract

Inspired by new designs, abstract forms and free style, these pieces have a strong character—some classic and elegant, others ethnic and spiky. Some of the models are discreet, while others are elaborate and futuristic.

Abstract necklace

This design is inspired by contemporary and stylized shapes. It works well with textured paper that is slightly thicker than usual.

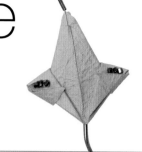

Making shape A

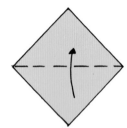

1 Fold one sheet in half along the diagonal.

2 Fold in toward the center along the dotted lines.

3 The model will look like this.

4 Reopen it and fold again along the dotted lines.

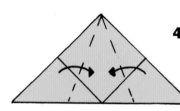

5 The model will look like this. Open the flaps again.

6 You'll use the creases you have made later on. For the moment, fold in the flaps again along the dotted lines.

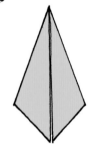

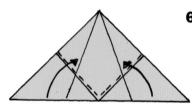

7 Fold out the flaps along the dotted lines.

8 The model will look like this.

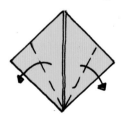

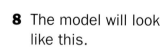

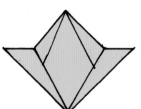

9 Reopen it so that you can see the creases made, then close again.

Materials

- 2 sheets of paper, 2¾in (7cm) square
- a pin
- a length of nylon cord
- 2 curved tubular beads
- glue
- a magnetic or screw-on clasp
- seed beads

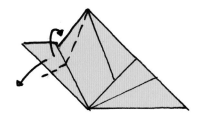

10 Fold back along the dotted line running down from the top point.

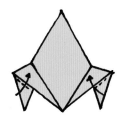

11 Pull the pointed flaps out slightly and fold them down behind.

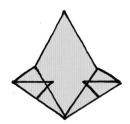

12 Fold the two small flaps over the front of the model. Your final piece should look like this.

Making shape B

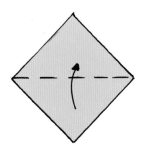

1 Fold the second sheet of paper in half along the diagonal.

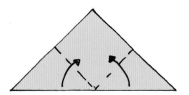

2 Fold in toward the center along the dotted lines.

3 Fold down the flaps along the dotted lines.

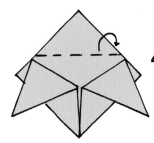

4 Fold back along the dotted line and turn the model over.

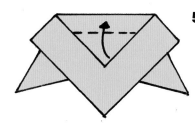

5 Fold up along the dotted line and turn the model over again.

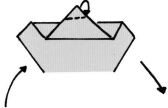

6 Fold the tip over the top of the model.

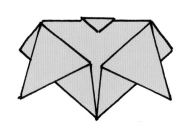

7 Your final piece should look like this.

Abstract necklace

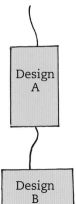

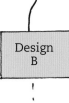

1 This is the structure you are aiming for.

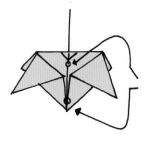

2 Using the pin, make two holes in shape B, as shown. Thread the nylon cord through this piece (it should be visible front and back).

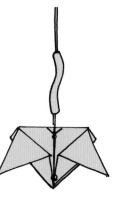

3 Thread the cord through one of the tubular beads.

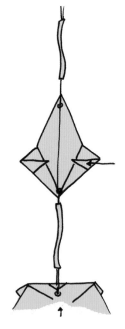

4 Glue the small flaps down on shape A to keep them in place. Now make a hole and thread the cord through this piece as you did with shape B. Thread the cord through the second tubular bead.

5 Complete the necklace with a magnetic or screw-on clasp.

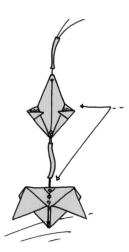

6 Glue on seed beads to decorate.

Contemporary bracelet

This pretty, modern piece works best using patterned paper.

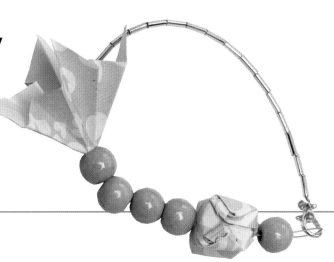

Making shape A

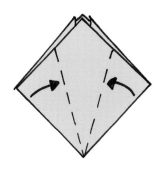

1 Start with a bird base, open at the top. Fold the top flaps to the center along the dotted lines.

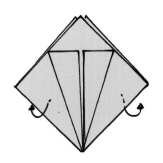

2 Turn the model over and do the same on the other side.

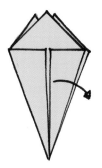

3 The piece should look like this. Open one of the flaps.

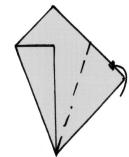

4 Inside reverse fold the flap.

Materials

- *2 sheets of paper, 2in (5cm) square*
- *a pin*
- *a length of nylon cord*
- *5 wooden beads*
- *bugle beads*
- *a lobster clasp*

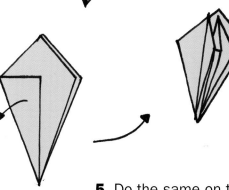

5 Do the same on the other side. The inside reverse folds should look like this.

Contemporary bracelet

Making shape B

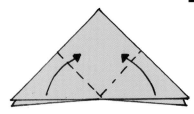

1 Using the second sheet of paper, start with a waterbomb base. Fold in along the dotted lines.

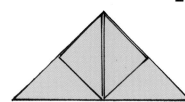

2 Turn the model over and do the same on the other side.

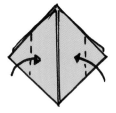

3 Now fold in the top flaps along the dotted lines.

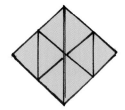

4 Turn the model over and do the same on the other side.

5 Tuck the top parts inside the openings of the flaps you have just made.

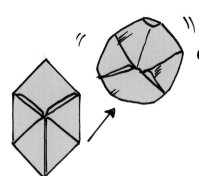

6 Blow into the model gently and inflate it to make a rounded shape.

Making the bracelet

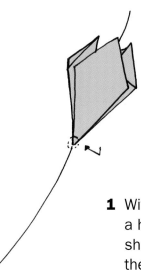

1 With the pin, make a hole in the point of shape A and thread the cord through.

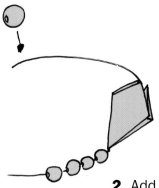

2 Add four wooden beads.

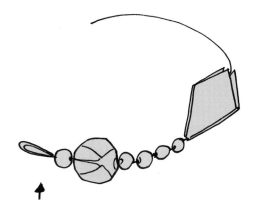

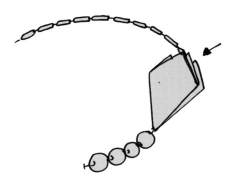

3 Make a hole in shape B and thread the cord through this, followed by the final wooden bead. Make a loop in the cord by passing it back through shape B and gluing it inside the shape.

4 Use bugle beads to cover the rest of the cord.

5 Attach a lobster clasp to the end of the cord, securing it with a knot.

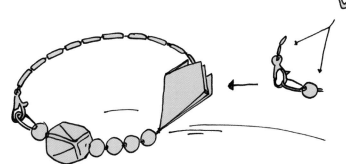

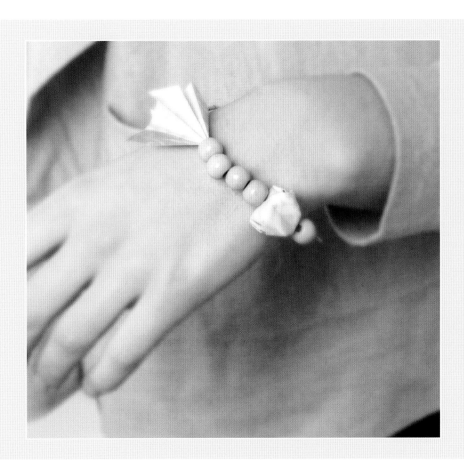

Abstract earrings

This is a simple but lovely design created with double-sided paper. Strong colors such as red or purple work well for these earrings.

Making the shape

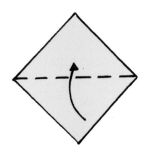

1 Fold a sheet of paper in half along the diagonal.

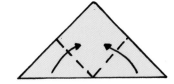

2 Fold in toward the center along the dotted lines.

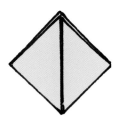

3 Turn the model upside down.

4 Fold up both flaps along the dotted lines.

5 Your model should look like this.

6 Fold down the tips along the dotted lines.

Materials

- 4 sheets of paper, 1.5in (3.5cm) square
- glue or double-sided tape
- a needle
- a length of nylon cord
- bugle beads
- wire earring hooks

7 Fold the flap up along the dotted line.

8 Fold the tip down.

9 Fold the remaining flap back at the center, shown by the dotted line.

10 Rotate 90 degrees.

11 This is your final design. Make another three shapes the same.

Making the earrings

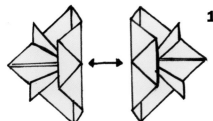

1 Position two of the pieces as shown.

2 Fix them together with glue or double-sided tape.

3 Using the needle, make a small hole in the top of the model and insert a short length of cord.

4 Thread it with one long or two short bugle beads.

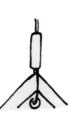

5 Tie the cord to an earring hook and finish off neatly. Make another earring in the same way.

Abstract bracelet

This design is minimal and contemporary and works well with single-sided paper.

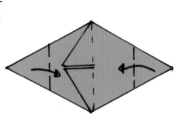

Making shape A

1 With a larger sheet of paper, start with a fish base. Fold along the dotted lines, as shown.

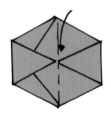

Materials

- *5 sheets of paper, 3.5cm (1.5in) square*
- *5 sheets of paper, 2cm (1in) square*
- *a length of nylon cord*
- *a screw-on clasp*
- *a needle*
- *glue*
- *bugle beads*

2 Mountain fold in half.

3 The shape should look like this. Now make four more.

Making shape B

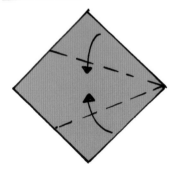

1 Take one of the smaller sheets of paper and fold along the dotted lines toward the center.

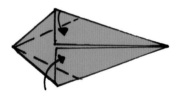

2 Fold inward again along the dotted lines.

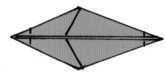

3 Fold in the tips along the dotted lines as shown.

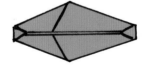

4 Turn the model over and rotate 90 degrees.

5 The second shape is ready. Now make four more.

Making the necklace

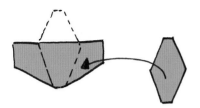

1 Glue shape B to shape A, following the outline, as shown.

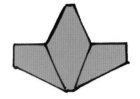

2 You will end up with five modular pieces like this.

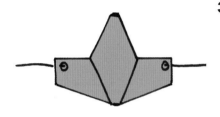

3 With the needle, make two holes on either side and thread the cord through.

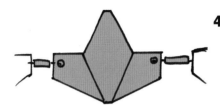

4 Thread a bugle bead on either side.

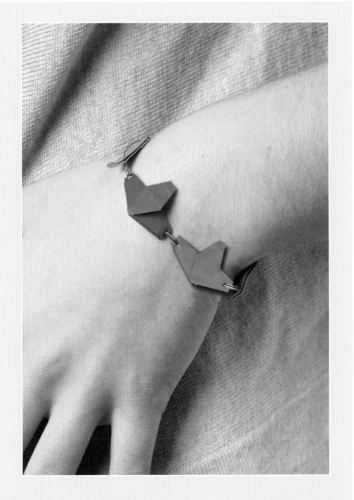

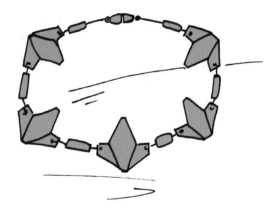

5 Keep going—your structure will look like this.

6 Attach a screw-on clasp and finish neatly.

Diamond necklace

This bold, elegant design is best made with washi paper.

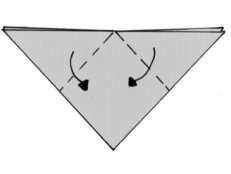

Making shape A

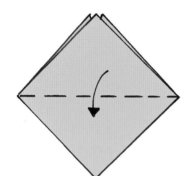

1 Start with a bird base, open at the top. Fold the top flap down along the dotted line.

2 Fold the side flaps in toward the center along the dotted lines.

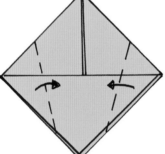

3 Rotate 180 degrees.

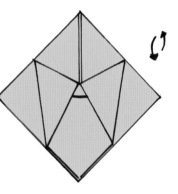

4 Your final piece should look like this.

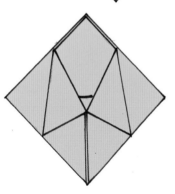

Making shape B

1 Start with a waterbomb base, open at the top. Fold the front flaps toward the center along the dotted lines.

2 Fold the remaining flaps behind along the dotted lines.

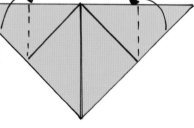

Materials

- 2 sheets of paper, 2¾in (7cm) square
- a needle
- a length of nylon cord
- a large bugle bead
- small assorted beads
- glue
- a magnetic clasp

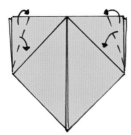 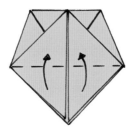 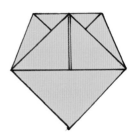

3 Along the dotted line, fold the top flaps forward and the back flaps backward.

4 Fold up the flap along the dotted line.

5 The final piece looks like this.

Making the necklace

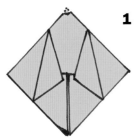

1 Using the needle, make a small hole in the top of shape A.

2 Insert the nylon cord, knotting both ends inside the model so that you have a double length.

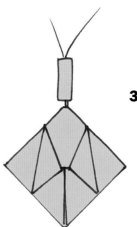

3 Thread a large bugle bead between the two origami models.

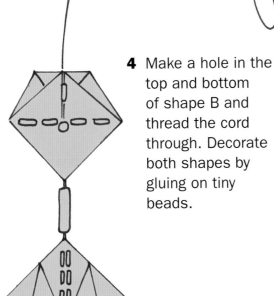

4 Make a hole in the top and bottom of shape B and thread the cord through. Decorate both shapes by gluing on tiny beads.

5 Attach a magnetic clasp to the ends of the cord and finish off neatly.

Ethnic necklace

This necklace is influenced by African design and works brilliantly with bright colors. You could use strong, single-sided origami paper; it also looks good made with patterned paper.

Making the shape

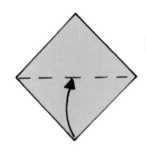 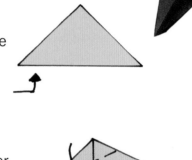

1 + 2 Fold a sheet of paper in half along the diagonal.

3 Open the paper and fold in along the dotted lines.

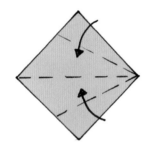 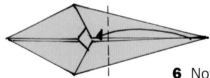

4 Fold in again toward the center.

5 Fold again, as shown.

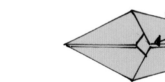

6 Now fold the model in half along the dotted line.

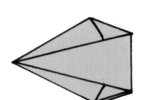

7 Rotate 90 degrees and turn the model over.

8 Your finished piece should look like this. Now make four more.

Materials

- 5 sheets of paper, 2¾in (7cm) square
- a length of satin cord
- glue
- 9 wooden beads
- bugle beads
- a magnetic clasp

Making the necklace

1 Position the first origami piece by threading the cord through the top, as shown (back view).

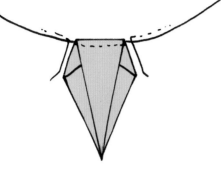

2 Add the other pieces, using glue to keep them in place.

3 Thread three wooden beads on either side of the origami—it looks good if the middle bead is slightly bigger than the others. Then glue three wooden beads and some bugle beads to the origami itself.

4 Tie the cord to a magnetic clasp and finish neatly.

Spiky gem necklace

Another African-inspired design, this can be made with any paper and works well with a large bead or gem in the middle.

Making the shape

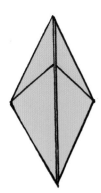

1 Starting with a fish base, press down the top part.

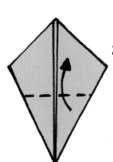

2 Fold up along the dotted line.

3 Fold down again along the dotted line.

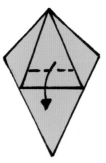

4 Fold the end up again . . .

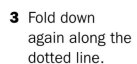

5 . . . and finally down again.

6 Turn the model over and do the same on the reverse.

7 Fold along the dotted lines and turn the model upside down.

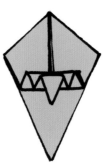

8 The final design looks like this. Make two more the same.

Materials

- *3 sheets of paper, 2¾in (7cm) square*
- *glue*
- *a needle*
- *a length of satin cord*
- *4 wooden beads*
- *a magnetic clasp*

Making the necklace

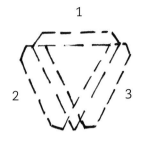

1 The structure is made up of the three pieces almost superimposed on top of one another.

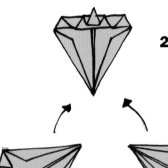

2 Glue the pieces together, following the structure above.

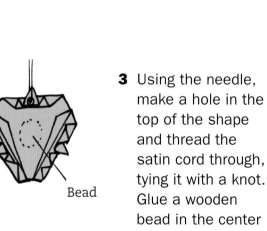

3 Using the needle, make a hole in the top of the shape and thread the satin cord through, tying it with a knot. Glue a wooden bead in the center of the shape.

Bead

5 Tie each end of the cord to a magnetic clasp.

4 Add three more wooden beads to the double length of cord.

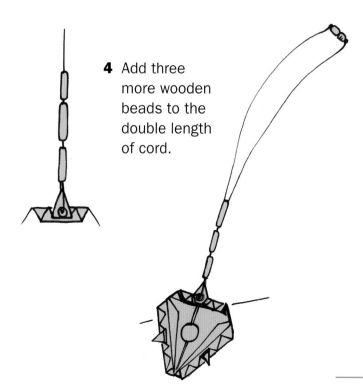

Spiky earrings

This design has a distinctive and contemporary look. It's best made with a strong, resistant, but fairly thin paper.

Making the shape

1 Start with a waterbomb base. Fold down along the dotted line.

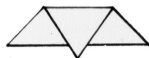

2 Flatten and open up the base.

Materials

- *4 sheets of paper, 1½in (4cm) square*
- *scissors*
- *a needle*
- *a length of nylon cord*
- *2 geometric-shaped beads*
- *glue*
- *wire earring hooks*

3 Press down the internal flaps.

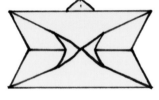

4 Rotate the model 180 degrees.

5 Fold along the dotted lines on both sides.

6 Push down slightly, changing the shape of the flaps on both sides.

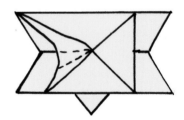

7 Cut along the middle line and fold down the paper, tucking it in.

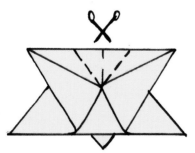

8 Fold up the point behind the model.

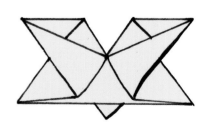

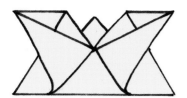

9 This piece is ready. Now create another one exactly the same. The two pieces make one earring.

10 Rotate and position the two shapes so that they are overlapping slightly. Glue them together.

Making the earrings

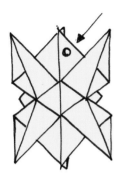

1 Using a needle, make a hole in the top.

2 Thread the cord through and add a bead to secure it.

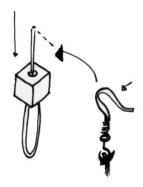

3 Attach the cord to an earring hook and finish off. Make a second earring in the same way.

Geometric & Boxy

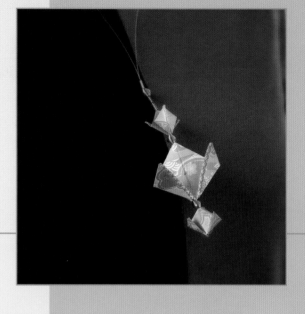

This last section is a celebration of geometry, using basic shapes to give form to interesting new pieces. Elegant and unique, they can be worn for fun or to impress a crafty audience! They are easier to make than they look and can be created in a wide variety of colors and patterns.

Box earrings

This design is inspired by the Japanese masu box and looks lovely made with delicate patterned paper.

Making the box

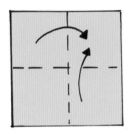

1 Fold a sheet of paper twice across the dotted lines and reopen.

Materials

- *4 sheets of paper, 1½in (4cm) square*
- *glue*
- *seed beads*
- *ear studs*

2 Fold all four corners to the center.

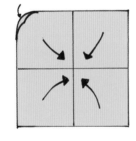

3 Rotate the shape so that it's square on.

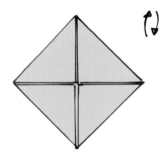

4 Fold in along the dotted lines.

5 The gap between the flaps should be about ¼in (5–6mm).

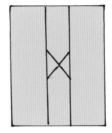

6 Reopen the flaps and repeat the folds on the other sides of the square. The square inside the dotted lines will be the base of the box.

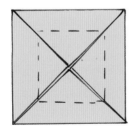

7 Open the side flaps and pull up the two still-folded sides to make the first and second sides of the box.

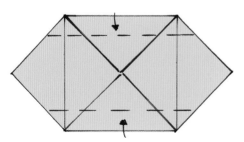

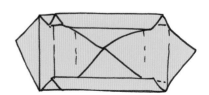

8 Start folding the left-hand flap in toward the center.

Box earrings

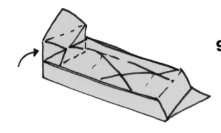

9 Fold the flap over and tuck it into the base of the box to make the third side. Do the same to make side four.

10 Turn it over—this is the top of the box earring. Follow the instructions for the boxes necklace opposite to make the bottom of the box.

Making the earrings

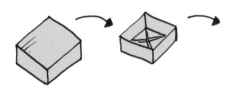

1 Fit the top and bottom of the box together.

2 + 3 Glue some beads on top as decoration.

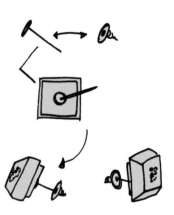

4 Glue the ear stud to the base of the box. Do exactly the same to make the second earring.

Boxes necklace

This project looks elegant and sophisticated and makes a lovely gift. The best paper to use is patterned washi. The necklace is delicate— you need to be especially careful when joining all the origami together.

Making the box

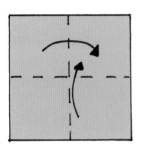

1 Fold the larger sheet of paper in half and in half again, as shown.

Materials

- *1 sheet of paper, 2½in (7cm) square*
- *4 sheets of paper, 1½in (4cm) square*
- *a needle*
- *a length of nylon cord*
- *2 long bugle beads*
- *a screw-on or magnetic clasp*

2 Reopen the paper.

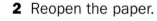

3 Fold all four corners to the center.

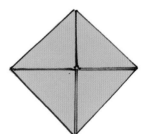

4 Rotate so that the model is square on.

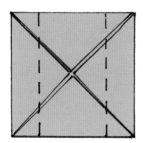

5 Fold both sides toward the center.

6 Make sure the sides meet, but they mustn't overlap.

Boxes necklace

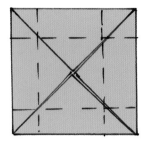

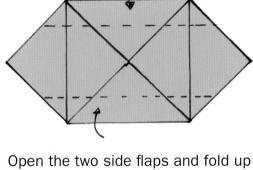

7 Reopen and repeat on the other two sides so that you have a square with clear fold lines.

8 Open the two side flaps and fold up the base along the lines at the top and bottom.

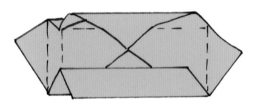

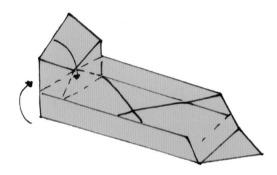

9 Holding up the top and bottom sides of the box with your right hand, fold the left flap in toward the center.

10 Fold the top of the flap down and close this side of the box. Now do the same with the right flap.

11 This larger box is the middle piece of the necklace. Make four more boxes exactly the same with the smaller-sized paper.

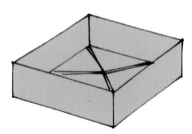

12 Using a needle, make two holes in the sides of each box, as shown.

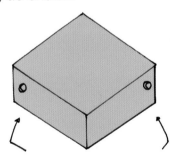

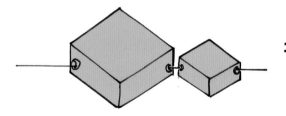

13 Pass a piece of nylon cord through the boxes, with the large box in the middle and two smaller boxes either side. Keep the boxes touching and add a long bead at each side of the arrangement.

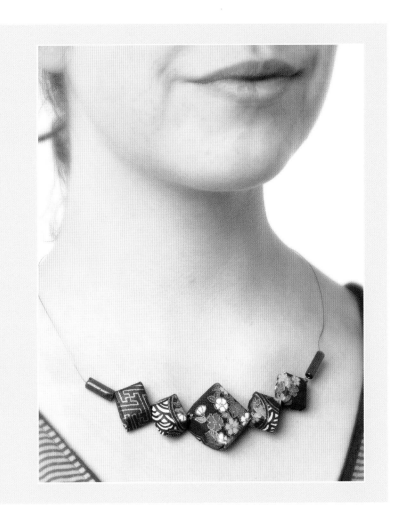

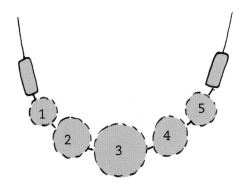

14 This is the structure you want to achieve.

15 Make a small knot on each side to keep the structure in place.

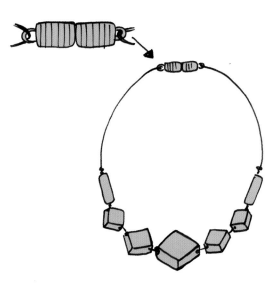

16 Finally, secure the necklace with a screw-on or magnetic clasp.

Aerodynamic earrings

This is a new design inspired by Futurism.
It can be created with any origami paper.

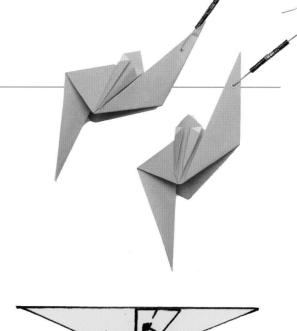

Making the shape

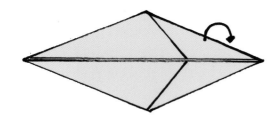

1 Start with a fish base, mountain folded.

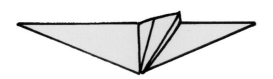

2 Fold in along the dotted line.

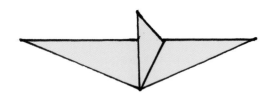

3 Reopen and start flattening the flap down.

4 Follow the creases you made earlier.

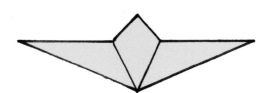

5 Turn the model over and do the same on the other side.

Materials

- *2 sheets of paper, 2¾in (7cm) square*
- *a needle*
- *a length of nylon cord*
- *bugle beads*
- *wire earring hooks*

6 Fold inward along the dotted lines.

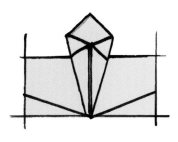

7 Turn the model over again and do the same on the other side.

8 The illustration, right, shows the detail of this design.

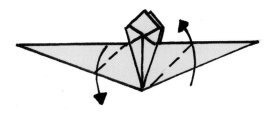

9 Following the dotted lines, fold down on the left and up on the right.

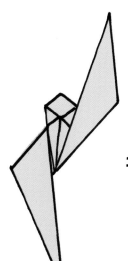

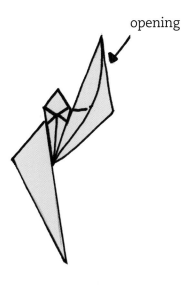

opening

10 + 11 Create an outside reverse fold on the right-hand flap and an inside reverse fold on the left-hand flap.

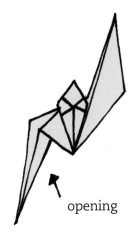

opening

12 + 13 Flatten the model slightly. Make another shape exactly the same.

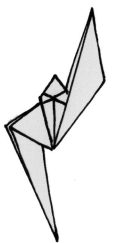

Aerodynamic earrings

Making the earrings

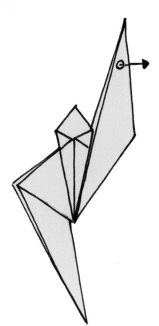

1 Using a needle, make a small hole in the top of the model.

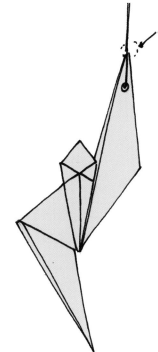

2 Thread the cord through the hole.

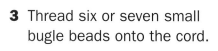

3 Thread six or seven small bugle beads onto the cord.

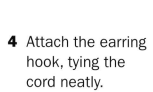

4 Attach the earring hook, tying the cord neatly.

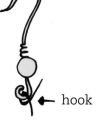

hook

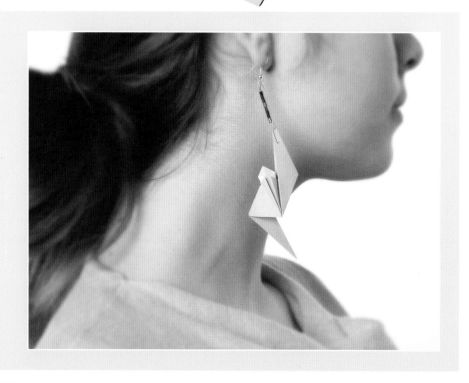

Chain bracelet

This is an interesting exercise in using very small origami. It works best with double-sided paper.

Making the chainlinks

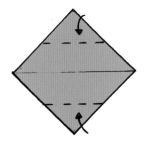

1 Fold a sheet of paper in half along the diagonal, then reopen it and fold along the dotted lines.

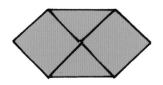

2 The shape should look like this.

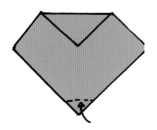

3 Reopen the bottom flap and fold up the tip along the dotted line.

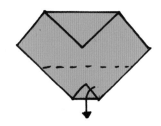

4 Reopen the last fold you made and fold the flap up again along the dotted line.

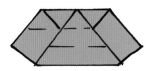

5 Reopen and repeat steps 3–4 with the top flap.

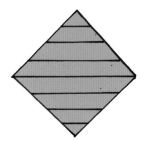

6 Reopen and turn the paper over.

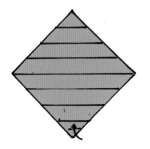

7 Fold the tip of the paper up along the line.

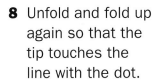

8 Unfold and fold up again so that the tip touches the line with the dot.

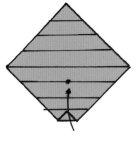

Materials

- *15–18 sheets of paper, 1½in (4cm) square*
- *glue*
- *a needle*
- *a length of satin cord*
- *a screw-on or lobster clasp*

Chain bracelet

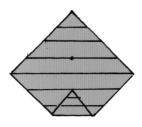

9 Unfold and repeat. The dot is higher up this time.

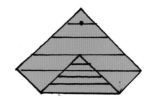

10 Unfold and repeat.

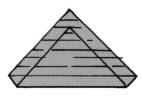

11 Repeat steps 7–10 with the top of the sheet.

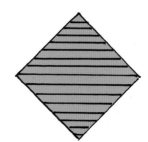

12 Reopen to see all the creases you have made.

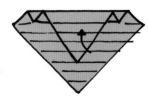

13 Start folding the top half like an accordion.

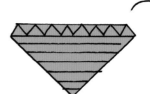

14 Do the same with the bottom half.

15 Once the paper looks like this, turn it over.

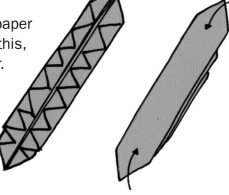

16 Bend the shape round into a circle and tuck in the ends.

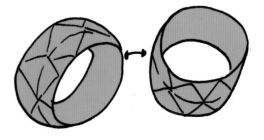

17 The final piece should look like this. Now create 14 more, or as many as you need.

Making the bracelet

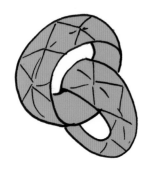

1 Start joining all the pieces, inserting one into the next and tucking in the ends. Use glue to secure the ends.

2 The chain should quickly start to take shape.

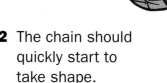

3 This is the eventual structure you want to achieve.

4 Using the needle, make a small hole in each of the final links. Insert a short piece of cord through each and secure with knots.

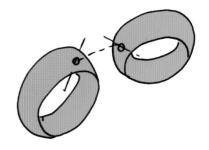

5 Add a screw-on or lobster clasp to complete the piece.

Piano earrings

This original design works perfectly if created using black and white double-sided paper.

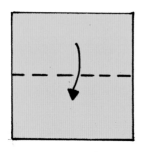

Making the shape

Materials

- 2 sheets of black and white double-sided paper, 1½in (4cm) square
- a black felt tip pen
- a needle
- a length of fine nylon cord
- seed beads
- wire earring hooks

1 With the black side facing down, fold the paper in half, as shown.

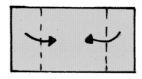

2 Fold in along the dotted lines and reopen.

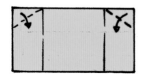

3 Fold down along the dotted lines and reopen.

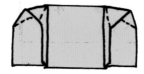

4 Open each of the end flaps and flatten them down.

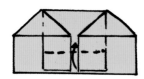

5 Fold the center flap up along the dotted line.

6 Fold it up again along the dotted line.

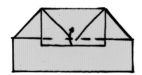

7 Fold it up in half again.

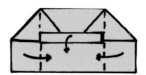

8 Fold the sides in along the dotted lines and reopen them slightly to make the two sides of the piano.

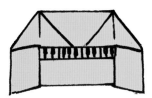

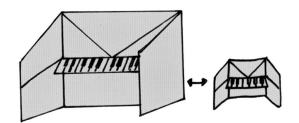

9 Fold down the small flap in the middle and draw piano keys on it with the black felt tip pen.

10 The final piece should look like this. Make another one exactly the same.

Making the earrings

1 Using the needle, make a small hole in the center top.

2 Thread through a short piece of cord.

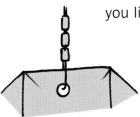

3 Add three small beads (any shape you like).

4 Tie the cord to an earring hook and finish off neatly.

Japanese fan necklace

This design is inspired by Japanese geisha fashion and works best if you use delicately patterned paper.

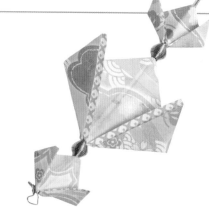

Making the shape

1 Using the large sheet of paper, start with a waterbomb base. Fold the top flaps in along the dotted lines.

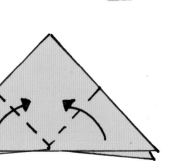

2 Fold the remaining flaps backward along the dotted lines.

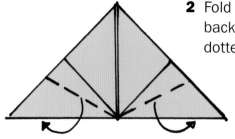

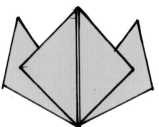

3 The model will look like this.

Materials

- 1 sheet of paper, 2¾in (7cm) square
- 2 sheets of paper, 1in (2.5cm) square
- a needle
- a length of fine nylon cord
- 3 spiral beads
- 3 bugle beads
- a screw-on clasp

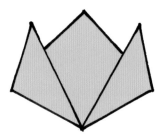

4 Turn it over. This is the finished model. Make two more the same with the smaller sheets of paper.

Making the necklace

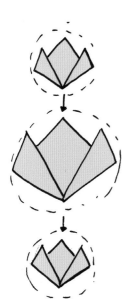

1 This is the structure you want to aim for. Using the needle, make a hole in the top of each origami.

2 Knot the cord at the bottom.

3 Thread one of the smaller pieces onto the cord, followed by a spiral bead.

4 Thread the large piece onto the cord, followed by another spiral bead. Then thread the second smaller piece and the remaining beads onto the cord. Tie a screw-on clasp to the ends of the cord.

Triangles necklace

This dynamic shape can be created using any origami paper.
I've used a fairly stiff type of paper here.

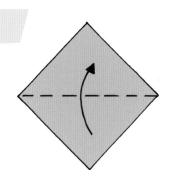

Making the triangle

1 Fold a sheet of paper on the diagonal.

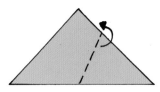

2 Fold behind along the dotted line.

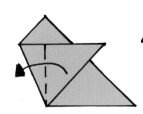

3 The shape should look like this.

4 Turn the shape over and fold the flap along the dotted line, as shown.

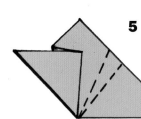

5 Repeat steps 2–4 with the other flap.

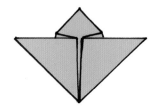

6 Your model will look like this. Turn the piece over.

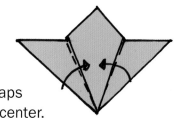

7 Fold both flaps toward the center.

8 Fold the flaps out along the dotted lines.

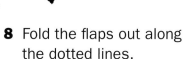

Materials

- 3 sheets of paper, 3in (7.5cm) square
- glue
- a needle
- a length of nylon cord
- bugle beads
- a spiral metallic bead
- 4 wooden beads, 2 light-colored and 2 dark-colored
- a screw-on or magnetic clasp

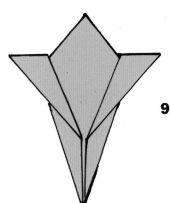

9 The final piece looks like this. Make two more exactly the same.

Making the necklace

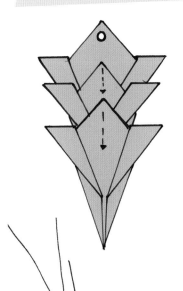

1 Apply glue to the three origami pieces and place them one inside the other as shown. Using the needle, make a hole in the top one.

2 Thread the cord through the hole.

3 Add four or five small bugle beads and a spiral metallic bead to the double length of cord.

light beads

dark beads

4 Add the four wooden beads, with the two light-colored beads in the middle.

5 Add a screw-on or magnetic clasp to the ends of the cord.

6 The final piece will look like this.

Triptych hairclip

This simple, elegant design works best using washi paper.

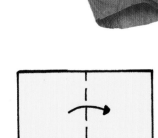

Making the triptych

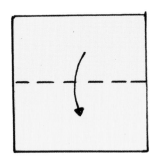

1 Fold the paper in half downward.

2 Fold in half again and reopen.

3 Fold along the lines toward the center.

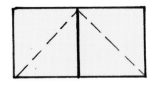

4 Your model should look like this.

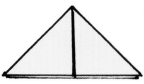

5 Turn it upside down.

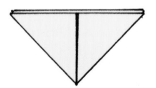

6 Open both flaps.

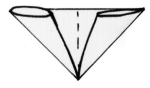

7 Press down, like this.

8 Make two more of these shapes exactly the same.

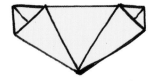

Materials

- *3 sheets of paper, 2in (5cm) square*
- *glue*
- *beads*
- *snap clip*

Making the hairclip

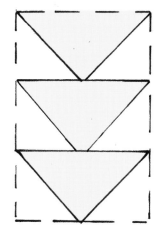

1 This is the structure you want to aim for.

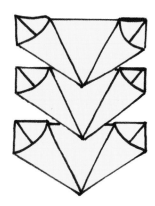

2 Glue the pieces on top of one another, overlapping them slightly.

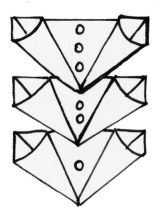

3 Add some round or square beads (or a mix) down the center.

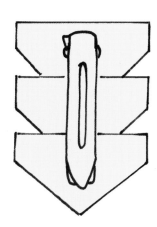

4 Attach a snap clip to the reverse, making sure it doesn't extend beyond the design.

Stockists

The following suppliers stock a wide range of materials for origami enthusiasts:

www.aliexpress.com/w/wholesale-origami-paper.html

www.foldedsquare.com

www.japancentre.com/en/categories/1057-origami

www.origami.com.au

www.origami-fun.com

www.origamipapermonster.com

www.theorigamipapershop.com

www.origamishop.us

www.paperchase.co.uk

www.thejapaneseshop.co.uk

The following suppliers stock everything you need to make beautiful origami jewelry:

http://m.pandahall.com

   Beads, findings, and gems

www.hobbycraft.co.uk

   Arts and crafts supplies

www.beadaddict.co.uk/

   Beads, findings, and gems

www.cooksongold.com/

   Precious metals and jewelry-making supplies

www.beadsunlimited.co.uk/

   Beads, pendants, findings, threads, and jewelry-making supplies